An Interlude of Time In America

By Charmiene Maxwell-Batten

An Interlude of Time In America

By Charmiene Maxwell-Batten

Copyright

ISBN 978-1-304-76243-6

All rights reserved. This work may not be copied, duplicated or imaged in any way, mechanical or electronic, without the written consent of the Copyright holder/author.

First EDITION 2013

Printed in USA

Contact:

Charmiene@hotmail.com

http://www.lulu.com/content/13922772

Books

By Charmiene Maxwell-Batten

A Medley of Reflections

Araminta's Message – a Communiqué from the Enchanted World of Fairies

Reflections of a Journey in Thailand and India

England – Ponderings and Reflections

Ponderings and Reflections of Childhood

Ponderings and Reflections of a Housekeeper

Switzerland – You Danced In My Heart

Sounds of My Soul
Sounds of My Soul volume 2

Finding My Moccasins
Windows on Life

Contents

Acknowledgements	11
Dedication	15
Introduction	17
HAWAII	
Surfing	29
Channeling	31
The Foot Reflexologist	35
Danny	39
The Enchanted Tree	43
In the Name of Divinity	47
ALASKA	
Anchorage to London	53
Five a.m.	55
Eskimos In Alaska	57
The Last Frontier	65
Sleeping Lady	69
Moonbathing	75
Sunsets	77
Nureyev	79
CALIFORNIA	
Dolphins	85
New Age	91

SEATTLE

Alive	97
The Singer	99
A Dollar	103
Ritzy's Red Earrings	105
The White Lotus	109
The Innocence of Kenny	113
I'll See You Again	117
A Mother	121
The Garden and the Concrete	123
Skipping	127
'Soul Retrieval'	129

TEXAS

Morning Warmth	141
Crash	147
Disappointment	151
Yolanda's New Shoes	157
Marshmallows	163
Noah's Ark	167
EPILOGUE-	169

There on the far ridge, ancient trees looming in the mist;
how old are you?

These Trees before me remind me of silent sentinels.
So, so still.

These silent woods. Ha!
The birds singing and river roaring;
how can I sleep?

HAIKUS FROM MONTANA
By Atmo Scott Leland

Acknowledgements

Thank you to LeRoy, for our home and Garden in San Antonio Texas. You know how much peace and fulfillment it gave me! It was also hard work during the dry summer months but nevertheless we created a haven.

Deep appreciation to my friends in Alaska, Hawaii, California, Seattle, Oregon and most recently in San Antonio Texas. You have all inspired my life!
Thanks to Leo for telling me to get rid of the excessive exclamation marks!

Many thanks to Ray Holland in Dorset, England. I am grateful for your help with Photoshop. Thankyou to Laura Redmond and David W. Morin Jr. for your kindness and help with formatting my books for IBookstores.
Thank you Marjorie Wallace for the photo of Pike Place Market. Thank you to Atmo Scott Leland for the beautiful Haikus and my heartfelt appreciation to Karen Young, Nicolette Lattanzio and Kaz Sephton for valuable feedback.
I also want to thank all the sages and philosophers who have over the centuries, shared insightful words of wisdom and hope - for all to read.

"At the touch of love, everyone becomes a poet"

Plato

*"If Laughter is crippled then tears are also crippled.
Only a person who laughs vibrantly can weep fully;
and if you can weep and laugh authentically –
you are alive!"*

Osho

*"We cannot despair of humanity
Since we ourselves are human beings"*

Albert Einstein

Dedication

Dedicated to LeRoy and Kali

Kali in Seattle

Introduction

An academic field research project took me to North America for one year. That one-year became several years as my assignment took a back seat and I found myself immersed in the metaphysical new age of spirituality. My scholastic commitment fell by the wayside.

Those first few years were partly beleaguered by an underlying yearning to resume the student life and complete a degree in Ethnology. In those moments of sadness, I deeply regretted having abandoned my studies and some cherished Swiss friends. I was often overwhelmed by a nagging sense of failure that took a few years to restore.

As it turned out, those years spent in America launched a period of exploration and expansion on many levels and for that I am grateful. The University of Life's teachings and all the soul searching that goes with it has its merits!

At an early and lonely stage of my life, writers like Anne Morrow Lindbergh and W. Somerset Maugham, both of whom wrote short non-fiction stories that provoked a deep reflection on life, had an impact on me. Their writing inspired me immensely and motivated an even greater curiosity in human nature.

This book is a collection of very human and personal observations while living in Hawaii, Alaska, California, Arizona, Seattle and most recently, Texas. In spite of years spent in North America, I retained a British accent and also expressed some added Swiss German characteristics that will remain an integral part of my personality.

A first impression of the USA was to be the Polynesian milieu of Hawaiian Islands. The nurturing effects of Hawaii are well known to many - a spot on the earth that emanates creativity. It was there that I developed a further interest and training in Kahuna medicine, astrology and palmistry. My ensuing work as a reader in the Waikiki International Market Place was excitingly busy. Greatly enriching my own knowledge in these areas, I worked and socialized with a group of healers, therapists and psychics. We were a multi-cultural bunch from all over the world, industriously involved in the health-giving aspects of humankind and the planet. Giving and receiving the qualities of relaxation, healing and optimism were all part of this experience.

The alluring Hawaiian ocean and all it encompasses deserves a mention. I was terrified at the prospect of immersing my face in water, ever since an incident in Spain, many years before when I was rendered powerless and dazed by the robust surf rolling me over and pulling me down to the depths. Gasping for breath and convinced I would drown on that beach in southern Spain - a phobia of crashing breakers ensued. Frequent trips to the warm Hawaiian ocean, while learning to surf and dive like a child again, all fears were released with the thrilling triumph at having overcome an impediment. A fresh new buoyancy permeated life in the wild ocean, once I faced my fears.

I drove a cheery red moped to and from my pretty rented cottage in the lush Manoa valley. The playful quality of life in Hawaii still affects people with a comfortable 'laissez faire' frame of mind. What a surprise when I decided to move to Alaska after two years in this island paradise. *Going with the flow* at that time, and always curious at the prospect of a new adventure, my friend Chinmayo convinced me to make this amazing transition. I left Oahu and arrived in Anchorage during the chilly month of October when people were dressed in gray and brown colors; their bodies seemed a little stiff compared to the smiling and noticeably stress-free body language in Hawaii. I felt I had arrived in a gray land - how wrong this first impression proved to be!

An intrinsic 'Yang' aspect of Alaska reflected a ruthless yet natural strength, expressed through a dramatic terrain of colors and climate. A quality of simplicity born of courage existed throughout this land. My Alaskan stories reveal the strength and fortitude that Alaska bestows on all who inhabit this magnificent terrain. I was especially drawn to Mount Susitna, which prompted the story of 'The Sleeping Lady'. A few years after leaving Alaska, I was to discover that my second cousin, Michael Baring-Gould lived in this Arctic state himself and taught at the University of Anchorage – he died in a tragic boating accident, the year that I arrived in Alaska.

I recall an excited phone call at midnight from a friend named Narayani. She had been driving home when she saw vivid pillars of colored lights beaming down to earth – the Northern Lights! Narayani said she was dancing in the lights and chose to share this blissful moment with me. What a beautiful visual picture she revealed on that auspicious night in Alaska.

A brief and unforgettable winter in Scottsdale, Arizona surrounded by huge brown rocks and fresh winter sun is worthy of mention. I love the glaring desert environment and the wilderness of a landscape that is rich in Native American symbols. I found myself connecting with a language that speaks of a time when wisdom was directly linked to the elements of earth. Huge red rocks in Sedona seemed to link the ancient past to a mystical future. A compelling feeling that interplanetary spaceships may have alighted is not unusual.

Moving to San Diego, and being immersed in the California 'new age' scene, a further and enthusiastic interest in alternative medicine grew. A sunny day in this surfer's paradise was certainly a place to savor life. Sparkling clothes effectively projected an image of a lighthearted California girl. Predictably, my narrative about dolphins was written during that time.

Remaining on the West Coast, the emerald city of Seattle brought new events into life. Many of the stories reflect my work as a holistic minded practitioner and metaphysical counselor during those years. I also worked in an herbal apothecary situated in Pike's Place Market; the renowned market where people visit from all over the nation and from other countries, to see the entertaining and notorious fish throwing activities. In fact, the fish throwers wrote a book, highlighting the art of laughter and joy as a means to energize and motivate performance in the work place. Many hotels and corporate companies now use this as a training module to enthuse their workforce.

After a truly breathtaking overland drive from Seattle to Texas, our arrival in San Antonio brought with it a desire to return to an 'ordinary' working environment. The allure of working in the alternative scene and the milieu of 'new age' had vanished – I wanted to do 'regular', down-to-earth work again. A delightful job as a front desk agent (hotel receptionist) at a beautiful hotel in downtown San Antonio was exciting. Never mind being up at four thirty in the morning to start my shift at seven, I was looking forward to the daily work. The hotel was in front of the famous Riverwalk, which is a picturesque river running through the city. Venice in Texas! On noticing there was a BURR Road in San Antonio, I wondered whether any relatives of my maternal grandmother, Florence Elvira Burr, may have settled here. I know that her two Great Uncles moved there from England in 1867, to start a sheep farm in Bee County.

Gardening became our passion after purchasing a house. I could hardly wait to get out and dig the neglected soil, plant flowers and bask in the Texan sun. We planted trees galore, purchased a few bird baths and invited wildlife into our small and thriving organic garden. Kali, our assertive sheltie, was even more motivated into chasing squirrels and birds around the garden, while I continued to write.

Kali in a field of flowers

Charmiene on Alki beach, West Seattle

HAWAII

"My candle burns at both ends,
it will not last the night,
but ah! my friends,
it gives a lovely light"

Fire and water collide with the power of nature; the Hawaiian Islands are born of geological violence. Standing 13,803ft above sea level when measured from its oceanic base, much of Mauna Kea is a dormant volcano. Mauna Kea is about one million years old, and thus hundreds of thousands of years ago it passed the most active shield stage of life. In its current post-shield state, its lava is more viscous. Late volcanism has also given it a much smoother appearance than its neighboring volcanoes.

In Hawaiian mythology, the peaks of the island of Hawaii are sacred, and Mauna Kea ("white mountain") is one of the most sacred. An ancient law allowed only high-ranking tribal chiefs to visit its peak. Ancient Hawaiians living on the slopes of Mauna Kea relied on its extensive forests for food. When Europeans arrived in the late 18th century, settlers introduced cattle, sheep and game animals, many of which became feral and began to damage the mountains.

SURFING

A wine cooler really did help me to stay on that surfboard!

Thrilled to have bought my very own surfboard, it balanced on the little red moped I drove to the beach almost every day, just like the other surfers. I wasn't really much of a surfer, not like my fearless friend Danya who could be spotted far out in the distance with all the other dedicated and resilient challengers. After just a few lessons, I surprisingly managed to stay on the board; that wine cooler helped. Being relaxed, a natural balance took over and even though I only caught a few baby waves, it was the feeling of being part of the trendy surfing establishment that was so motivating. Chatting with other surfers gave me a sense of pride; bruises on my hipbone earned by paddling out to the waves on a rigid surfboard, further assured my surfer status. It was wonderful.

Driving to the North Shore numerous times with my friend Amalin, we found golden sandy beaches and intriguing rattan-constructed shops selling colorful beachwear. Able-bodied surfers catching enormous and powerful breakers on their long and short boards. Those able bodied surfers could be seen in the distance, gliding swiftly and ecstatically like dolphins on the crest of the wave. Though graceful and exhilarating from an onlookers' angle, it required enormous concentration and control to stay on the wave; I would have liked to find the courage to do this myself. Immersing my head underwater remained a scary prospect for a few months. These Islands certainly helped me overcome my fear. When the warm blue ocean embraces one's body daily, it becomes a friend.

One of the numerous lessons for me in Hawaii: *'Catch the wave while it's there'!*

CHANNELLING

Celebrities have written about their supernatural experiences. Several channelled books offering up-to-the-minute words of wisdom had suddenly emerged; the channelled language of Emmanuelle and Ramtha were branded around as a prophecy of knowledge from higher entities, voiced through the ether. It was the latest trend in metaphysical circles.

During the 1970's, I attended a spiritualist church on several occasions in England, where mystical messages from long gone relatives, were being relayed to the congregation through mediums. Friends and loved ones who had passed on to the other side, seemed very chatty. Bringing closure and consolation to aching hearts was a great comfort to many in this gathering. These spiritual mediums were homely, elderly people and there was a comforting ordinariness to the whole setting.

In Hawaii, on the other hand, mediums were extraordinarily colorful and their gatherings were highlighted with a touch of contemporary showmanship - it was Hawaii!

A woman in her thirties channelled a lively spirit named Aurora. Natalie Shipton was a down to earth ex-therapist who became very popular in the metaphysical community. Her numerous workshops, classes and sessions to enhance intuition and psychic ability were available for purchase after the meeting. Although many open minded and enthusiastic scholars of the intuitive arts were thrilled with the classes, I found the instruction dull and predictable. It even seemed repetitive and hollow. The participants, however, were filled with awe and a childlike eagerness, which warmed my heart. Someone once said that it is the faith you have in something that creates the trust and manifestation.

The 'A team', a trio of mediums who were certainly an attention-grabbing and lively crew of individuals, rode around on sleek silver mopeds. Calmly suave on their space-mobiles, one could spot them driving majestically around Waikiki and Manoa valley. One member of the trio channeled an alien who communicated from aboard his spaceship. The human 'channeller' underwent a total character transformation as the spaceman spoke through him.

Another member of the 'A team' was a conduit for fairies. She actually didn't speak any known words or identifiable language; it was 'fairy talk'.

While being receptive to supernatural messages, my playful and adventurous friends enjoyed these activities with the added and levelheaded capacity not to be ensnared by any dogma; there were others in the audience who seemed quite somber, taking things very seriously while seeking to analyze and label these newly formed ideologies.

Merriment enhances life, why waste a minute being unnecessarily solemn. It's not a shallow amusement that I speak about but an option to choose a cheerful stance rather than a gloomy outlook. Enhancing insight without becoming weighed down with a rigid belief system is a quality that strengthens inner and outer vitality.

I was interested and curious at that time about the channeled words of Edgar Cayce; it seemed that a lot of knowledge and uncanny astuteness regarding medical treatment and health issues had come through in the form of channeled information; it was a thought provoking area to explore.

As quickly as the clairvoyant entertainers in Hawaii appeared, they rapidly vanished! A few of them remained and their books emerged to satisfy the reader's appetite, but the frenzied craze for mass channelling evaporated.

There's a recent innovative interpretation emerging, with the success of a television host, John Edwards, who effectively brings messages from 'the other side' to individuals who have lost loved ones. Numerous mediums are now attempting to follow this example. Money making is a lure in any situation where entrepreneurs willingly arrive to satisfy a public craving. There are mediums and marketers now as there were decades ago who provide a bridge between two worlds. Visionaries will continue to exist in the future until perhaps one day, all humans will use and exercise an innate ability and wisdom with which to connect to the unseeable. Humans will one day own up to their inherent capacity to trust the unknowable. Will we then need oracles?

Perhaps this knowledge and understanding is already embedded in what is known in science as 'junk DNA'. It has been said that this unknown and as yet unencrypted DNA holds the coding for the future evolvement of mankind.

THE FOOT REFLEXOLOGIST

I first discovered this extraordinary woman by reading a booklet, which was an intriguing source of information about foot reflexology. The book was sold at a popular health food store in Manoa Valley; the author had written, printed and distributed her handbook at wellness centers all over the island. Sprinkled with humor and empathy, the content of the paperback was informative and sparked an immediate impulse to contact the author, ultimately leading to my weekly sessions in foot reflexology.

My health at the time was vulnerable, and this small, dark haired woman from Hawaii was the start of a step-by-step journey to different healers and authors of herbal medicine.

My strength was not only restored but also better than it had ever been in my teens and twenties. During my visits with this lady, ironically, she cheerfully chitchatted while her children played and the TV reverberated with non-stop sounds. None of that mattered or invaded the soothing sanctuary that enveloped me. Her comforting voice came clearly through any other sounds while therapeutic hands worked deftly on the pressure points on my feet. Sinking into a relaxed semi-slumber, I left feeling revitalized after each session.

On my recommendation, some friends who were sincerely interested in the alternative health field went to see her; they were distracted by the outer stimulus and reverberation in this surrounding. It's true, during her sessions' one could hear a television in the adjoining room and her children would wander around while she was massaging feet and maybe she did look a bit scruffy – these were clearly not outwardly impressive signs of a practitioner. Perhaps my friends sought out a more conventional set-up. Yet I knew without doubt I had found a healer and I wasn't disturbed by her outer appearance. We all find our healing in whichever way we are guided to do so. Perhaps this foot reflexology was simply suited to me. I felt at peace there, and have never since, found a foot reflexologist with such a gift.

This willowy woman didn't charge money to those individuals who could not afford to pay because her prime objective was curative. She volunteered and offered her services at the local hospital. She taught classes. She truly loved and believed in her work. People even brought animals to her - pouring into her humble home at all hours with their sick pets.

In the following years, I was to encounter some charlatans in the alternative health field who wore white coats and had an office that exuded the right image. Alternative and holistic health practitioners who display a professional medical appearance may certainly inspire apparent confidence with a selection of electrifying jargon and techniques. Alas, a mere façade of expertise is often enough to impress most people. The small Hawaiian lady made no pretense, no special mystical veneer, no white coat or sales pitch, just a simple, ordinary and caring woman whose spirit resides in a place of integrity. I knew she was unusual. I was grateful to have discovered her, and glad that my body had found healing through her exceptional work. Sometimes the real pearl is to be found in the most unusual and unexpected places.

Listening to the signals of our body, exemplifies a simple wisdom; the mind, on the other hand, is impressionable.

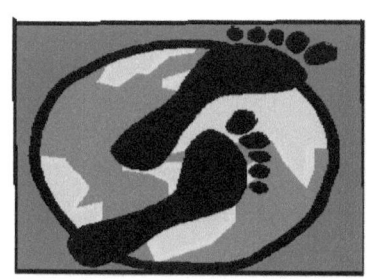

DANNY

Flamboyant and intelligent, Danny's Portuguese descent endowed him with dark glinting brown eyes and chiseled looks.

Exploring all the newest locations around Waikiki for our late night dinners and snacks was an entertainment in itself. Fascinating bistros, local small eating-places, ethnic cafes, expensive, Avant gard restaurants and of course the wonderful all night café, 'eggs n' things' - we discovered them all and fervently perused their bill of fare. Meals with Danny were unique escapades filled with animated conversations that motivated us both with new and bright ideas. Our own personal and colorful lives at that time were topics of intense discussion and our aspirations were thrashed out with fervent excitement.

The presence of Danny in my life was a constant reminder of a vital and guiding principle - the wisdom of playfulness! He was and still is a positive and uplifting human being, who encourages anyone who happens to cross his path with inimitable optimism. Filled with an inspirational drive, he was certainly a central part of my life in beautiful Hawaii.

Danny attended the University of Hawaii where he studied psychology and later went on to work in the prison as a counselor for anger management. His individual studies with Louise Hay and Elizabeth Kubler-Ross enriched an inherent gift as a healer. His talent went beyond psychology.

Interested in human behavior, he had an uncanny knack of reaching out to people on all levels. It was very easy to relax with Danny and being vulnerable was never a weakness in his eyes. People opened their hearts to him; even the most hardened and embittered humans found a way to expose their anguish, to become softer and ultimately find joy again.

The day we went horse riding on the Big Island of Hawaii, I overlooked my fear of horses amongst all the uncomplicated laughter and lively incidents. I still have a photo of Danny fearlessly cavorting across the river on his horse, arm in the air while shouting gleefully across to us. I was sure he would fall off and into the gushing river. He didn't!

My vivacious friend Danny is compassionate, perceptive, childlike, wise and sensitive. Sharing some wild and unique moments is an experience never to be forgotten.

An existing and contemporary approach to life with regard to healing physical and life-threatening sickness - is through laughter. I read of the circumstances where a man cured his cancer by spending six months laughing in whichever way he could. He bought amusing videos, watched comedies and learnt to laugh again.

After emerging from the innocence of childhood, very few adults can truly release the depth of spontaneous and heartfelt laughter. It's recently been scientifically established that a state of authentic cheerfulness, physically changes the cellular structure in the body so that cells grow to be robust and healthy, thereby deflecting disease. In contrast, negative emotions such as depression, anger and sadness can affect the cells of the body in such a way as to induce illness. I believe that Danny has the gift of healing through sharing his bright and curative laughter.

Danny continued expanding his studies and today his humanitarian spirit is boundless as he continues to share his unique rays of celebration.

"I like people who make me laugh
I honestly think it is the thing I enjoy most – to laugh.
It cures a multitude of ills.
It's probably the most important thing in a person
And it's wonderfully infectious"

Audrey Hepburn

THE ENCHANTED TREE

A beautiful Banyan tree with huge strong roots grew within the famous Waikiki International Market Place. Like a bazaar, the open market was filled with multihued Hawaiian souvenirs and gifts to entice the travelers who came flooding into this Island paradise. Handcrafted items including jewelry, novelties and artwork were available in plenty. Tee shirts, with bright colored Hawaiian themes and fashionably casual clothes as well as accessories, flashed alluringly before one's eyes.

Delicious ethnic food items were also for sale - my favorite was the fresh coconut milk, in a coconut.

Nestled in a corner of the bustling market place, a thriving enterprise with Intuitive Readings had been assembled around the Banyan tree. Two large comfortable wicker chairs were placed in the small sanctuary and soft flowery curtains provided discretion. The name of this establishment was aptly named 'The Enchanted Tree'. I was very fortunate to be one of a group of empathic readers working on a well-organized time Rota, where lines of people waited eagerly to have a ten-minute reading. I thoroughly enjoyed this lively and rewarding work where for a moment in time, I was drawn into the personal and intricate lives of individuals and visitors. I found myself recognizing the tough challenges that many people from all walks of life were courageously facing, though outwardly it was not always obvious. Most vacationers were excited to know about the emotive theme of love and marriage in their life. While doing my best to respond with integrity, I found myself encouraging a tangible groundwork for a constructive future rather than allowing predictions to become a potential escape from reality.

Being an intuitive and responsive listener, I had the utmost respect for other individuals who had the ability to predict future, but for me, it was of greater value to provide a place where people gain insights into how their lives may be freed from unwarranted burdens. Following the direction of Swiss psychologist Carl Jung, I favored developing an interactive approach to the symbolism of Tarot Cards. Fortuitously a receptive audience was open to the prospect of positive living in the here and now, as opposed to mere fortune telling.

On those lovely hot days of summer, my thirst quenching 'Emperors choice' iced tea and some tropical fruit to snack between readings, provided all the sustenance I needed. Hawaiian music cascaded from the restaurant above as the hours flew by until my friends met me with surf and boogie boards, for an exhilarating dip in the ocean.

On our initial arrival in this tropical oasis, Muriel, my Swiss friend, and I found casual work handing out flyers to tourists in Waikiki. Flyers advertising boat cruises to the excited vacationers was one of many jobs offered to those adventurous travelers who first came to Hawaii, seeking out a means of living there. It was fun and sunny work that motivated an outgoing and sociable milieu.

After that, began my gratifying and intriguing work under the Enchanted Tree.

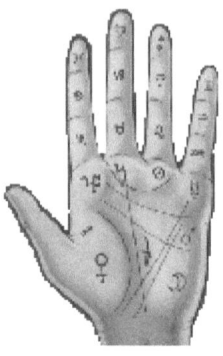

"What lies behind us and what lies before us
Are tiny matters compared to what lies within us"

Oliver Wendall Holmes

IN THE NAME OF DIVINITY

The aggression that passionately drives humanity to defend and fight for an individual God, their God - is an enigma.

Most Spiritual teachers have over the centuries, pointed in a direction towards peace and harmony. Such prophets of wisdom have touched the very heart and soul of mankind, yet once they died, an elaborate foundation was built around the imprecise leadership of their ardent followers. By manipulating and even misunderstanding the very words of their teacher, tenure and dogma soon replaced the original vision of awareness.

Countless examples of ghastly behavior demonstrated by devoted individuals, who were followers of a religion, can be found in historical accounts as well as in current reports.

There are horrifying narratives about Christian missionaries, who evidently displayed depravity and cruelty towards Africans, Native Americans, Eskimos and Hawaiians. Spanish Christians apparently cut off the hands of South American inhabitants who would not convert over to Christianity. It was a gruesome structure of control, based on coercion and terror.

Centuries ago in 'civilised' Europe, wise women were burnt at the stake for ridiculous and bogus reasons.

Catholics and Protestants demonstrated brutal warfare in Ireland. Israeli and Palestinians continue their fight. There are curious contradictions such as Tibetan Buddhists who are not permitted to kill, even a flea or a tapeworm, though they will eat meat that's killed by others. Followers of some more current spiritual groups appear to have discarded one set of rules only to replace them, unsuspectingly, with new rules.

There is a distinct sense of power, control, ownership and self-righteousness, where each religious conviction appears to feel that their own belief system is the right one, which seems to justify doing anything 'for the cause'. Numerous religions appear to believe that it is God's way, to kill the enemy.

Who is the enemy?

I personally believe that God/Life/Existence is everywhere and everything. It's not a competition, nor is it a justification to commit acts of cruelty.

Many people express a great respect for life and the freedom from man-made doctrines as well as the profound courage to find spirituality in their own way. Those who seek advice in a harsh and challenging world are slowly waking up to the need for insightfulness rather than submissiveness, which is heartening and hopefully liberating.

*"If the only prayer
you ever say in your life
is thank you.
It will be enough"*

Eckhart

ALASKA

"Thankyou whistled the wind.
Thankyou rumbled the ocean,
and the words echoed from every mountain top"

"One just has to have a rest
and be ordinary.
Be natural
– that is the zen approach"

Osho

ANCHORAGE TO LONDON

Due to a prohibition of passage over the USSR during the cold war years, all European air travel heading to and from Japan was directed through Alaska. Anchorage became a stopover, an exhilarating interlude from an otherwise lengthy sixteen-hour journey. Hotels with modern facilities and magnificent views had been built to accommodate countless aircrews as well as passengers.

During the 1980's, Anchorage, capital of Alaska, embraced an International ambience while blending the intrinsic and earthy wildness of the Northern territories. This worldwide affinity for a global edge made for an interesting stopover. A harsh and stunning environment where daring and determination proved to be a vital component was an added attraction to many who wished to make this stopover.

Flights to and from Europe always brought a sense of excitement to many travelers. Flying for hours and hours over snowy untarnished terrain, my world became brightly white for eight hours. It was an extraordinary flight over the North Pole where mountains resembled crystal pinnacles resplendent in their uniqueness, yet merging as a symphony of harmony and light. A golden sunrise as well as a dramatically vivid sunset displayed in the vast expanse of sky, deepened the majestic view. No nighttime, no darkness! I was convinced that Apollo, the Greek Sun God, raced through the skies with his chariot - the airplane following close in his tracks. Mesmerized, I could hardly take my eyes away from this spectacular scenery. The lure of food at mealtimes was no contest.

Sadly, this flight is not made anymore. The underlying reasons for this change hopefully indicate steps towards a more peaceful world - the end of the Cold War. There are no more direct flights from Europe to Anchorage over the Pole; the airlines take an alternative route. Those long European flights heading for Japan are now routed over the USSR.

FIVE A.M

One early morning I had reason to drive out to the Army base just outside Anchorage. It was five a.m.

Everything was still and pure. The cold air, silent as roadside trees stood splendidly, covered in white powdered frosting. Driving slowly and carefully on the sleek icy roads gave me an extra opportunity to marvel at nature's magical work of art.

Awestruck at the soundless beauty surrounding the wide empty highway, I became acutely aware of a godly paintbrush where spectacles of inspiration are exquisitely painted across the land - for us mortals. Living works of art that allow the human spirit to pause for a moment in time, while recognizing a collective and deep-rooted wish to bask in serenity. I basked in it as an awareness of universal love filled my heart.

Peace permeated my soul when I drove in those early mornings. Nothing moved outside. A stirring glow of inner warmth flooded through me.

That was twenty years ago. Things may have become a little busier by now.

> *"The freedom you look for,*
> *is where you look from."*
>
> – Jac O'Keeffe

ESKIMOS IN ALASKA

Sometimes intoxicated and sleeping on the pavements or else propped up against substantial props, indigenous Eskimos lingered around the city's ambiguous Fourth Avenue. Wintertime was no exception to this demonstration of a people who definitely don't appear to be in their element anymore. An environment that must have felt hostile to the original inhabitants, Anchorage was filled with scenes of unnatural dejection during the mid and latter years of the 1980's.

Like fish out of water, numerous native Alaskans seemed lost and often disorientated in their own town. Those who hung out day after day, night after night on Fourth Avenue, were often labelled slow, witless and scruffy. This, I suppose, is the way they must have appeared to a society who saw themselves as superior to the indigenous population.

During that time, it was hard to find an Arctic inhabitant on the stylish Fifth Avenue just a parallel street over. The modernised Fifth Avenue, boasted select department stores, shopping malls, tourist attractions as well as avant-garde restaurants and bistros. Bistros offered whole roasted garlic with French Brie - I enjoyed the newly opened and fashionable 'Sachs Fifth Avenue' restaurant.

Actually I did see some Eskimos on Fifth Avenue who were 'suitably' dressed in western garb. Their appearance and manner revealed prosperity. I met an educated and cultured man of unmixed arctic origins who owned a shop on Fifth Avenue, where he resolutely stocked exclusively native, handcrafted items. Those items were true works of art, embodying an authentic mark of Inuit culture. It was certainly a tourist attraction and the appealing items were beautifully made, incorporating the traditions and history of an ancient society. The man explained that this was his way of giving back some dignity to a race of people that were in danger of losing their legacy, their culture - and their land.

While browsing in his shop, the present dilemma of the native population presented itself spontaneously in our conversation; he related an incident that touched me very deeply. A local Inuit man, a simple man whom he knew well, had been thrown in jail by the local police - for being drunk. With sadness and profound empathy, the narrator revealed the plight of this captured person who simply did not understand or know why he had been incarcerated. The shop owner visited the jailed man a few times but could do very little for him in a society where rules and policy are so different to the indigenous culture. Indeed for someone who has descended from a race of nomadic human beings that roamed the vast and exposed Northern plains of Alaska in absolute freedom, a tribe of people who demonstrated the very spirit of courage - such prison bars served only to stifle and extinguish that fire of life that had sustained him and his people for generations. *"We die in captivity"*, said the shop owner, who was a full-blooded Eskimo himself and understood the heart and soul of his people.

Western 'civilization' introduced alcohol as a sociable enterprise - perhaps unknowingly, certainly mistakenly. Where the western physique generally stomachs liquor fairly well - the physical make-up of the indigenous population does not tolerate intoxicants. This may be the reason I saw listless and inebriated bodies lying around the streets.

Implanted in this cosmopolitan setting, they were so far removed from a way of life, lived for generations; their hereditary constitution was in jeopardy of being forced onto submission by the threat of a new and perilous lifestyle. The spirit of the native population was being broken. It was a tragedy and deeply traumatic.

Historic Eskimo tradition incorporated the very courteous action of a man offering his wife for the night, to an esteemed visiting guest. This was a sign of polite behaviour towards his neighbour, and I do believe that the wife considered it to be acceptable herself. I had never heard or read of distressful responses to this gesture. The customary words conveyed in this ritual were: *'Would you like to laugh with my wife'?* Surely this is an inoffensive statement that indicates happy sentiments. Alas, in the days of the missionaries, civilised man reproached this practice while branding it barbaric and evil. Eskimos' gradually ceased their inherent custom of decorum, in deference to a new way – the way of modern man. Maybe they had no choice. There are numerous reports relating to the unkind and ruthless treatment of human beings, by missionaries who regarded these enduring Arctic residents as unchristian. I assume that the Eskimos' believed their mentors and the customs they were teaching would represent principles worthy of aspiration.

As history unfolds, the advent of ruthless, avaricious, money hungry white men arrived - not missionaries one would hope. Rough, insensitive white men snatched these arctic women and raped them. Rough pioneers boldly and forcibly raped their way into the Arctic land and its' people. I am sure there were no happy and light-hearted sentiments to be experienced in this deed. To be told not to share your wife in laughter and gladness because it was sinful, and then to have their wives brutally and cruelly seized by those very same people, must surely have been puzzling.

During the 1960's a hospital had been built in Alaska to accommodate and provide medical treatment to the native Eskimo population, free of charge. Perhaps those business men who discovered rich, dark oil on the natural and pristine slopes of Alaska, may have felt the need to offer the indigenous dwellers of this land some meager compensation? Guilty perhaps at having snatched not only their land with its abundance of oil, but to have wrenched away their whole way of life.

I don't believe there is a conscience implicated in this 'altruistic' gesture - a calculated and political manoeuvre would seem closer to the truth. Another compensation for the theft of this land involved the lavish reimbursement of monetary gifts; modern gadgets were being purchased with all the funds that had suddenly descended on the Eskimo population. Snowmobiles were now strewn about this untouched landscape - motorised vehicles racing across the snow, were being driven primarily for pleasure and speed. Snowmobiles were discarded and left to rust when they no longer worked and the terrain began to resemble a used car lot while defiling a stunning land. Snowmobiles in exchange for their land - does that really sound like a good substitute? In the beginning, I don't think the natural inhabitants pursued the lure and complexities of cash as the Western world has done for centuries. Their society was based on kinship, bartering and a community spirit. The inherent method of transport across the plains had been dog sleds. I have no doubt that an awareness of the care and conservation required by these dependable modes of transport, was apparent and moreover, performed with excellence. Mushing is mainly a tourist attraction now - an entertaining souvenir.

There is one last aspect of historic Eskimo culture that I feel worthy of mention, not only because it stirred me profoundly, but because it reveals the fearless courage of an exceptional race of people when living in their natural environment. As an Eskimo aged in days gone by and was consequently unable to keep up with the rest of the group across a merciless terrain, the older person would declare that it is time to 'Walk into the snow'.

Walking deliberately and alone into the snowy horizon, the elderly individual left the group without once looking back. In this sentiment I am reminded of the grace and dignity that is a distinct attribute of the human spirit. The Eskimos' themselves saw this ritual as an act of divine faith. They were in fact walking towards God in that moment. Confident in the knowledge that their God welcomed them after a life of merit, honesty and strength. I do believe that missionaries could possibly have learned some wisdom from Eskimos'.

"The shoe that fits one person, pinches another,
There is no recipe for living that suits all cases"

Carl Jung

THE LAST FRONTIER

This name itself invokes a sense of thrill - as though one has made it to the end of the earth, which in some ways is true.

During the Cold War years this land was obviously the last frontier before the emergence of Russia on the other side of the Bering Sea; a massive gathering of United States military was clearly endorsing this statement.

Alaska was and still is known as the Last Frontier. A place where the quality of life is wild, simple and authentic.

When Russia and the U.S grew to be less intimidating to each other, things became a little more relaxed as demonstrated in a New Year's presentation held at the newly opened Performing Arts Center in Anchorage. Indigenous Eskimos from both sides of the once impenetrable barrier between Russia and the USA were now performing together on stage. It was an indication that the two armed countries had finally relaxed their dividing wall of threat. For now anyway.

There was a feeling of celebration, because the Arctic population was not being forcibly separated anymore. It had been an unnatural and long severance of this Nordic race, and now they all seemed relieved at an emergence and indication of peace.

The show itself was exciting, although the Americanized group of Inuit performers seemed more simulated, as though posturing and even craving acknowledgement. The Russian group of Eskimo performers, on the other hand, immersed themselves entirely in their performance, singing and dancing with abandon. This unreserved passion coupled with precision and talent was immensely inspiring to the spectators. I personally love watching Russian ballet dancers for that very reason. It was remarkable to see this ambiguous characteristic displayed here - two sides were of the same inherent race yet the differences were evident even though the parallel ethnic group had been outwardly separated and shaped by two different societies.

This entire performance imparted a quality of profound unison, joyful inspiration and cultural pride – there were many clear moments when the audience saw and felt that spark of recognition and inherent unity in this noble and ancient civilization - that had been temporarily and painfully separated.

Be a writer,
Find a quiet place,
use a humble pen.

Paul Simon

THE SLEEPING LADY

Bootleggers Cove is an entrancing location in the city of Anchorage. Residing there in a building with stunning and uninterrupted views over Cook Inlet bay, and a direct view of the magnificent Alaska Range, it felt sacred to me. White pinnacles generously bestowed throughout the land were 'crystal palaces' that imparted a majestic enchantment across the bay. Just a glance at the Alaska Range sparkling on the horizon would leave me with a sense of awe and exhilaration. Immersing oneself in this commanding view was a priceless encounter.

Located to the right of this vast panorama was the 'Sleeping Lady', a spectre of untroubled and placid presence and my constant companion for two years. A fleeting glimpse was enough to fill my human soul with contentment. Mount Susitna indeed resembles a sleeping lady.

Alaska itself is a land where the timid and fainthearted may not flourish. A territory demanding courage, determination and endurance - virtues that are rewarded a thousand fold by this land itself. The harsh terrain invites an abundance of outdoor ventures throughout the year. Hiking up snow driven hills in winter is both exhausting and splendid at the same time. Evening skiing, surrounded by the haze of blue luminous lights is breathtaking. Mushing through the snow with eager dogs at the helm or ice-skating at the local University leaves a sparkle in your soul. Various outdoor water pools that turn into hard ice as soon as October heralds the arrival of freezing weather - the long winter unapologetically steps forward with resolve. Climbing and clambering up into the hills once the frost melts down will reveal brown sharp rocks and cycling along the inlet with the midnight sun shining boldly into one's face during the precious summer months, will electrify one's senses.

During the annual fur rendezvous, crowds from far and wide mingle eagerly together amongst all the festivities. Historically, it was a meeting of trappers to sell furs or purchase supplies, and to splurge and celebrate. The renowned Iditarod also taking place every February is thrilling, and, at times, sad. Excited and resilient dogs always ready for the expedition ahead of them probably had no idea of the hardship they would encounter. Primed and eager to set off with a sled of supplies for the thousand-mile trek to Nome, their enthusiastic barking certainly added to the anticipation of everyone around. The likely death of some of those dogs during their long and exhausting odyssey always brought sorrow to the whole community. It certainly brought tears to my eyes.

The presence of black and brown bears often spotted approaching and appearing in the city of Anchorage, keeps the human population alert. Numerous and hair raising encounters of humans and bears in the outer regions of this state were recorded in stories, songs and personal experiences. There were plenty of moose, an animal resembling a horse and a reindeer, seen in the woods and the bicycle trails around Anchorage. Never very far away from the townships, they even came to munch tree foliage in my friend's garden.

Mount Susitna actually does resemble the reclining form of an Eskimo lady clothed in her snug and thick garments of natural origin; very fitting in a land of snow and ice where Eskimos' are the true dwellers of an extraordinary and awesome territory. There does in fact exist an interesting and poignant legend relating to this mountain – a fable that has been passed down through the generations by word of mouth. It is a love story between a young man named Nekatla and a young woman named Susitna. She lay down and went to sleep waiting for her love to return from a dangerous mission. When news of his death reached the village, the villagers could not bear to wake Susitna from such peaceful sleep. They wove a blanket of soft grass and wildflower blossom and gently laid it over her: 'May you always dream of your lover' they prayed.

Today Susitna still sleeps through the seasons, dreaming of Nekatla. In winter she is covered by her snowy quilt, in summer you see her resting beneath a green and flowered blanket. It is said that when people of war change their ways and peace rules the earth, Nekatla will return and then Susitna will awake.

Perhaps another visit to 'The Sleeping Lady' will be reminiscent of the haunting tale and the peace that this mountain exudes.

Many people have pre-conceived qualms and doubts about life in Alaska. Having lived there for five years I regard it as an experience of enormous worth, filled with memories of a land vibrant with life. Wintertime with its ruthless weather conditions was unquestionably fortifying and invigorating. I loved it! People grow healthy and strong; I believe I was one of those many people who fall in love with Alaska. Someone once said of Alaska that mankind has not been able to harness or ravage this untamed land - I wonder why!

I will always remember the tragic incident that caught my attention in 1995. A British female mountain climber who had two young children at home in Britain lost her life in an avalanche on the exacting K2 Mountain in India. She had been the first woman to complete the ascent to the peak of Mount Everest successfully without oxygen. Her husband, in a television interview, explained earnestly that she always chose to live her life according to this ancient Tibetan saying:

' It is better to live one day as a tiger,
than a thousand years as a sheep'.

Surely this portrays the spirit of Alaska and all those who choose to live there – including myself.

"The mountains, trees and rivers change their appearance
with the vicissitudes of times and seasons,
as does mankind change also with their own experiences
and emotions"

Kahlil Gibran

MOONBATHING

Bathed in a soft blue glow I awoke one night to see the moon gleaming through my window. Indigo light was shining on my face on that ice-cold night at one o'clock in the morning. It felt peacefully blissful - there was no other way to describe the effect it had as I found myself stretching out and savoring the glow.

Sleeping by an open window with the frosty clean air on my face, I was snug in a bed covered by lots and lots of cozy comforters. After that, as long as the night was clear, I lay in deep untroubled slumber as the open window invited a radiant moon to come shimmering into my bedroom.

Rekindling a long forgotten light that resonates within our innermost soul – 'moon bathing' gave me a feeling of renewal and since that time, looking into the night sky to see a shining moon is a reassuring indication of luminous and munificent light. This glimmering globe forever beaming down on us mortals seems like a treasure in an often discordant world.

That very first and unexpected encounter with the moon in Alaska was an enriching occurrence that has continued to be a lingering and soothing event. Seeing that soft glow now evokes a comforting memory of a benevolent blue light that gently touched my face.

When moments in life seem dark and difficult, a reminder that a soft and loving radiance is within reach, to ease the gloom that can weigh heavily on our sensitive and oh so mortal heart.

SUNSETS

Glowing above me was a flaming sky ablaze with deep orange hues, heralding the unique brightness of an Alaskan sunset.

Strong vivid colors swathe and leap across every one of the happy shoppers outside the local supermarket as faces alight with the sparkle of a Nordic sky. A sparkle that is known to all those of us who have lived in Alaska! Those bright sunsets uplift our human spirit while renewing the pure trust in a divine strength. Many people wonder about those dark winters until they themselves witness the dazzling revelation that Alaska truly reveals.

Fiery red and orange splashes, thrown across the sky from a pot of celestial paint announced summer sunsets over Cook Inlet. Flaming colors transmuting into rich deep purple by midnight - it never grew dark at that time of the year.

As evening unfolded a huge luminous moon could be seen hanging low and daringly over the pastel pink and twilight-tinted mountains.

Walking onto the veranda on a late summer evening, I was always reminded that Alaska displays some of the most dramatic day's end I have ever seen. When asked how I coped with the dark winter months in Alaska – what would you say? I believe it is a well-kept secret. How I miss that arousing twilight finale.

"Sunsets are so beautiful,
That they almost seem as if we were looking
Through the gates of Heaven"

John Lubbock

NUREYEV

"He knew that he had to dance to the end
– and he did"

While living in Alaska during the late 1980's I had the exceptional opportunity to see Rudolf Nureyev dance in person. Being a role model for many young and aspiring dancers - I know that the fiercely impassioned and roguish face had captivated me for many years.

After reading his biography in the 1970's, the imprint of this man who relentlessly spent his youth reaching for the height of his art and indeed attaining it was extraordinary. I was in awe of him!

When Nureyev came to dance at the Operahaus in Zurich in the 1970's, there were countless and delighted descriptions from people who said that: *"He flew"*, *"He challenged gravity"!* It was evident that his skills as a dancer, his charisma and the impact he made was exceptional. I had not seen him then and regretted it terribly.

It was 1989 when I finally saw him in person, at the newly built Performing Arts Centre – the pride and joy of Anchorage, Alaska. He came with a group of French dancers from Paris. I had the good fortune to have a prime seat bought for me by a reckless and extravagant American friend who embarrassingly cheered and shouted during the ballet as though it were a football match. This same flamboyant man bought a ticket for me to attend the reception and mingle with the dancers after the performance.

Sitting quietly in my expensive seat, I was enveloped with eagerness while awaiting the moment for him to come on stage. It was a dream coming true.

He appeared at last, a stocky man in his fifties whose body was clearly unable to fly or defy gravity anymore. I suddenly felt the sadness of our bodily existence, followed by a profound compassion for the collective human predicament of ageing. Nureyev's body was not permitting him the physical expression of a spirit who soars to the skies, wild and free! I was acutely aware of the reality that encompassed a corporal world.

After this initial and poignant revelation I watched him dance. Affected even more deeply and fascinated at the same time, I knew that the dancer himself was absolutely present.

At the reception there were masses of strawberries covered in white chocolate; it was a sumptuous feast and the mood of excitement rippled throughout the room. I was restless and excited to see this man close up, the man who had been an icon to me for most of my life. Being aware of this secret wish, my brazen American friend promptly took me right over to face this much admired legend. Bashful, yet filled with admiration, I was speechless; no words came out but I did look into his eyes.

There was no mistaking his fiery essence. A spirit undeniably alive and sparkling. Ageless! I do believe that he did defy a material world by retaining his impassioned life-force in spite of an ageing and constricting body. In my view he conquered the limitations of being imprisoned in bodily form.

A young body is capable of expressing the depths and heights of passion in its most exalted and physical way, an ageing body on the other hand can make a powerful impact with magnetic intensity. Not so obvious to the shallow eye!

A wild untamed spirit was still alive within Nureyev's body.

He died a few years later. An extraordinary man, an outstanding dancer and a legend that will remain in my memory.

"How can we know the dancer from the dance"

William Butler Yeats

CALIFORNIA

"April hath put a spirit of youth in everything"

William Shakespeare

My beloved Sheltie - 'Passion'
In San Diego

DOLPHINS

Perhaps it was California popular with its New-Age inclinations, or possibly a collective realization and sensitivity of many at that time who chose to focus on healing a planet. The topic of dolphins had exploded into our consciousness, becoming a trend. One of the peak experiences many wished for was to swim with dolphins – an event that alerted the entrepreneurs to cash in. Dolphin channellers were all the rage and dolphin therapists assisted children and adults to regain physical and emotional health.

A mingling of people with a spiritual and metaphysical perspective on human aspirations was plentiful in this small and busy surfers' paradise on the Southern Coast of California. Ambitions of corporate affluence exhibited by those of a more material inclination were concentrated in other areas.

Even the cafe nearby aptly named 'Miracles' in Cardiff-by-the-sea, always seemed to abound with lively faces, multi-coloured clothes, relaxed laughter, and, above all optimism. Sitting in the sun, munching my healthy sugar-free muffin, I felt part of the 'nirvanic' culture.

Aside from this currently popular and genuine kinship being expressed towards the world of dolphins, there really was a deep affinity towards these gentle and beautiful creatures. Dolphins have been known to rescue humans from drowning and most recently utilized to cure people's depression and mental illness. Dolphins give themselves willingly and lovingly to mankind.

Many dolphin-friendly pals at that time did much to promote an awareness surrounding commercial tuna fishing, even reaching the political domain to express their concerns. Feeling a distinct inclination to be a part of this movement in a more individual way, I enlisted in a demonstration at the harbor, protesting against the slaughtering of Dolphins. In my view it was brutal and unnecessary – we all felt that such carnage was preventable.

Another exceptional event during this time was the discovery of Sea World, though not in the usual approach, as a tourist. Having bought annual membership tickets to Sea World, we joined a group of dolphin loving human beings who went to Sea World every single day, year after year. It was a commitment and an act of love with the exclusive intent, once through the doors of Sea World, to head directly to their dolphin friends who were confined in a concrete pool. As soothing human arms were gently immersed into the water, the dolphins recognized their allies – at that moment a unity of two species connected in a bond of tenderness. The exuberant marine creatures rushed over to welcome their pals as the sensitive converging of human hands and dolphin bodies met in a profound and mutual acknowledgment. The four friends tenderly befriended and comforted any new arrivals in the enclosed pool; these dolphins clearly hungered for this heartening camaraderie.

Surrounding the pool were crowds of noisy visitors teasing the dolphins by dangling 'bait' bought from the tourist shop nearby. Evidently such bait was a useless attempt to entice them over. Some children even tried to grab the dolphins in a self-absorbed craving. Parents allowed and even applauded this apparent lack of sensitivity; perhaps the children hadn't been shown any other way of treating our fellow inhabitants of this planet.

The friends, on the other hand, attracted dolphins like bees to a honey pot - talking and laughing with their marine buddies for two or three hours. They had no need to tempt such intelligent, sentient beings with trivial 'bait'; the offer of affection was more appealing. These caring visits surely kept the dolphins from dying out of sorrow in their cramped fishpond.

Equipped with a season ticket, we learned how to greet these creatures with respect and above all love. A calm meditative quality was needed for the dolphins to become accustomed to a new person. They recognised their human friends by a feeling that was transmitted through the water. We immersed our arms and simply waited without expectation; it is one of those manifold occasions where the act of grasping does nothing but deflect the very object of desire.

Scott attracted one young dolphin who nudged gently at his hand and then lay back revealing a soft white belly; finally he seemed to indicate his wish that Scott should jump in the pool and play. Our friends laughed and talked with their dolphin friends, each forming a particular friendship with one or the other. The dolphins reciprocated with warmth – an obvious link between two realms was established as the hours sped by. I imagined that human relationships could very well flourish more than they do by gleaning and integrating this essence of purity and playfulness exhibited by dolphins.

This same group of friends would go for a dip in the ocean very early in the mornings, often sighting dolphins while swimming out towards the deep sea. We joined them on a rugged uncrowded beach in San Diego as they pulled on their wetsuits and dove into the breakers with laughter and delight. That morning I was close enough to see sleek, ebony bodies gliding in unison through the waves as seven or eight dolphins were making their way across the bay in a wild and graceful movement. The intrinsic nature of freedom was being displayed before my eyes. A tear welled in my eye as I remembered those beautiful creatures in a concrete spherical pond; watching the wild dolphins coasting along in harmony, I was acutely aware of the disparity.

Six months prior to these events, not knowing how he would deal with a powerful and difficult situation in his life, Scott had been resting meditatively on a tranquil beach in the early hours of the morning. While sitting quietly on the sandy shore, he impulsively looked up to see three dolphins surfing with ease and vitality towards him. As the dolphins came closer – and seemed to be attracting his attention, his thoughts swiftly and inexplicably turned to a new sense of understanding and his feelings suddenly became clear.

This phenomenon brought us in contact with those mystical creatures who are overflowing with love. Perhaps mankind may not have yet fully perceived such love as conceivable.

NEW AGE

I would best describe the New Age as a movement to establish a broader spiritual outlook on the very nature and aspirations of mankind. A perspective involving a conscious and honest view of man's body and soul in unity, encompassing ways in which people may live in harmony with themselves and others. There is no doubt of the existence of numerous, varied and subjective views, opinions and perceptions of the concept known as 'New Age'.

While living in Hawaii, Alaska, California, Arizona and in Seattle, it was evident that in all of these places the New Age movement, offering alternative as well as historic skills to the field of healing, counselling and spiritual concepts, was a positive and flourishing part of the community. Actually, though heralded as the New Age, many aspects were traditional and ancient practices, now emerging with a fresh and innovative approach.

The spectrum of advisers in this line of work are diverse, ranging from academic professionals to gifted psychics and healers, all mingling collectively in a unified ambition to restore health, awareness and peace to a somewhat ailing planet.

In California the innovative trend is inundated with practitioners to a point where it's overcrowded; I would love to see the overflow move into the other more rigid parts of America where a diversity of choices would prove valuable. Parts of America are confined strictly to a rigid, dogmatic and even man-made Christian approach. There are people living in a stern and self-righteous way while often reprimanding and reproaching themselves and others; imitating the method and words of some nineteenth Century American missionaries, they seem very harsh. It certainly prompts the question, 'what became of the original teachings of Christ who rescued a prostitute from being stoned by the so called righteous people; A Christ whose teachings were loving, non-judging and above all compassionate?'

Christ is depicted in pictures as a sensitive and gentle person whose facial expression is tenderly benevolent. Yet I've been shocked to see the aggressive and ominous faces of mortal and contemporary preachers who dominate their congregation with fear and control. What became of these original teachings that were filled with wisdom and guidance?

Perhaps California, renowned for its unconventional and broad-minded inhabitants, is a nucleus and a mecca for those seeking this broader approach to spirituality; a way of thinking which embraces much of the insightfulness surrounding ancient long-forgotten knowledge. But even New Age healers, psychics and practitioners have a penchant for buzzwords, dogma and crusading, coupled with skilled marketing.

"Truly I say to you that thoughts
have a higher dwelling place than the visible world"

Kahlil Gibran

SEATTLE

Charmiene and Kali, Alki beach

"Love has the same relationship to the soul,
as breathing has to the body"

OSHO

ALIVE

Covered by a thick layer of numbness, are there people who seem to have hidden their life's vitality? Or is it lost? Others may try to share a spark of life, a ray of hope, a sign of joy – and still there is no indication of life.

Buds bursting through a honeysuckle plant; dew laden leaves shining through the morning sun like little crystals - the fragrance of a gardenia in full bloom – these are life's gifts that enrich and renew vivacity while setting off a contented smile that stretches across faces and hearts.

What earlier and emotional injuries occurred in those human beings who cannot share in such wonders – what happened to them and when? Wounded souls who seem to engulf those moments of magic into a pool of numbness, even through the convincing veil of a good-natured smile. Those people who put a damper on things, perhaps unknowingly – would they engulf my own sense of wonder and reduce me to a glum blob of flesh, unable to find excitement or joy in anything anymore?

Is a sense of childlike wonder truly enriching? Perhaps 'these' people I so easily critique and even fear have their own passions and joys, which may be more deeply and quietly expressed in ways I may never understand. Wishing to explore and embrace passion in their own private way, those people may not wish to share such feelings.

Human emotion is a mystery – surely we can bridge our misunderstandings and misconceptions of each other with heartfelt generosity and empathic communication? Learning about the mysteries of another human being with receptivity, rather than assuming that everyone has to be the same, would be the manifestation of a conscious world; a world where we each acknowledge the color and fragrance of this diverse and wonderful garden of flowers called humanity.

I want to understand this state of numbness that I sense in some people, while at the same time maintaining caution so as not to be engulfed into a black hole and lack of sensation. I love being alive!

THE SINGER

Photo by Marjorie Wallace

Pike Place Market is an attention-grabbing tourist attraction in Seattle; a market characterized mainly with the busy trade of fish, flowers and produce. Strolling around the intriguing shops or being entertained by street musicians and performers, visitors almost always include this place in their sightseeing agenda;

En route to buying my favorite drink, a hot chai at Starbucks, I heard a voice singing as though the sounds were reaching out to the Olympian Gods; to this day I can still remember the remarkable sound of a young boy singing. I heard and saw him only two times in the Market.

I was mesmerized by the exquisite voice of this twelve-year-old singer who didn't display any glitzy facial expressions or hand movements and no stage tactics to distract from the pure and heavenly voice. His vulnerable and timid willingness to be here in front of us, gained the admiration of many. Arms lying limply at his side, there was just a divine voice in an unassuming body. He sang like a nightingale. Tears welled up in the onlookers' eyes as they listened. They too were overwhelmingly touched by the extraordinary and yet simple presence of a child whose pale apprehensive face was compelling.

He gave so very much of his energy to us, his audience, as he hastily grasped gulps of water between songs. I felt an urge to call out to him: *"There's no need for you to exhaust yourself or hurriedly and apologetically drink water between songs; you truly have what it takes to be a great artist – please take your time to drink and rest"*.

I remained silent and quietly acknowledged his music as I recalled an experience the year before where somebody's pampered young daughters were playing the piano in their affluent home. With all the manicured showmanship of classical performers, their recital was flawless and rang of perfection. They were not thirsty or in need of water, nor were they exhausted. They were calm and composed in a luxuriant setting. Yet it felt unnatural and even contrived. I was not moved…my heart didn't dance…. I was bored at being duty-bound to sit and admire a performance that had not arisen from freedom but instead, a display of parents proudly showing off their 'talented children'.

Such young girls behaving as though they were adult concert pianists seemed grotesque. Where were vulnerability, courage, and innocence? Who had stolen it?

My heart opened with tears of joy at the sight of the pale skinny little boy in Pike's Place Market who sang so courageously in order to collect money for Conservatory training. He earned his audience.

To have heard him sing was an honor and unforgettable moment. I knew that one day he would bring bigger crowds to tears…one day very soon.

"A bird does not sing because it has an answer.
It sings because it has a song."
~Chinese Proverb

A DOLLAR

I was waiting at the Bus Stop one morning when he politely asked for money. Instinctively I turned away and ignored him. Rejecting this small and unassuming bearded man who came up to me with his placid request, gave rise to a growing discomfort in my stomach; I felt sad as I watched him walk away.

With an unpretentious magnetism, there was something out of the ordinary about him. It may have been his demeanor or his bright eyes that caught my attention; I had the distinct feeling that I was seeing an ageless leprechaun.

Feeling strongly and curiously compelled, I hurriedly took a dollar bill out of my purse and walked steadily towards him, gladly handing him the cash.

His face or was it his spirit suddenly lit up as he thanked me. I felt more like thanking him.

After a few moments, he walked by me with a light-footed spring in his step and a beaming face. Hardly noticing anyone else around, he seemed absorbed in his own world. *"I'm going to **Sit'n Spin** for a coffee"* he muttered with a smile.

Sit 'n Spin, an uncommon and arty Café/Laundromat nearby is a place to sip coffee and tea while doing some laundry in downtown Seattle and chatting with an eclectic group of students, artists and backpackers is always a fascinating diversion there.

Walking towards 'Sit 'n Spin' as though he was jaunting off for the day with plenty of money in his pocket, he certainly gave me a feeling of pleasure.

Watching the bright man stride away with a skip in his step...... I felt happy. Then my bus arrived.

RITZY'S RED EARRINGS

My head was stuffy and I felt dazed that morning; the noises of the marketplace and the minutiae of worry were exhausting. Focusing on the present moment was not effortless. Curiously, those cheerful sounds in the market place were usually enlivening, but that day I was out of sorts. I went to Starbucks for a Chai with my Zany friend Ritzy.

In that instant Ritzy's untainted voice came through clouds of abstraction as she said with excitement:

"Look at my earrings"

Bright red bunches of cherries were hanging from her ears. It seemed humorously light hearted and within a split second I was back again in the present moment, all haziness gone. Laughing with fresh vitality, I wondered why people spend so much time utilizing intricate and often tedious techniques in order to re-discover their present moment, when in reality it may be remarkably uncomplicated.

I recalled a situation in an Ashram in India many years ago when crowds of Westerners arrived for meditation and training groups; it became a little overwhelming for those of us, a small group who had been there during the quiet Monsoon interlude. A dear friend told me that he looks at people's feet when feeling flooded by copious faces and crowds, which brings him to the clarity and calm of the present moment. He said that it drains energy to look blankly into a throng of nameless faces, especially when any form of personal communication is absent.

When the pioneering and adventurous Ritzy blew into my life I found myself gadding about town and socializing. Ritzy is a journalist, writer and world traveler who's unconventional and forward thinking ways are refreshing to her friends.

Later when relating to her how much her comment had prompted clarity and laughter, she said quite simply: *"I just wanted you to see my new earrings"*!

The clammy tentacles of ego did not stick to her; a bird flying through the skies of life leaving no footprints and following no footprints. A bright and free soul.

We were both aspiring writers at the time, discussing creative topics and the meaning of life as well as commiserating from time to time on the harshness of this worldly existence; yet nevertheless recognizing the brilliance of a beautiful planet and of humanity itself. Memories of happy and youthful years at University were regained in those meetings. I felt immersed in the magical and creative world of intellect and academia when on an outing with Ritzy.

Exploring restaurants was not only entertaining but also a mission of investigation. Savoring the most appetizing cheeses from Italy, France, Switzerland and England – downtown Seattle became an exercise in sampling cheese plates!

With striking crystal chandeliers hanging from the ceiling of the Four Seasons Hotel, we enjoyed a luxurious high tea in the ornate tearoom. It was a childlike and untroubled world for a couple of hours. I was reminded of the times in Hawaii, when Danny and I explored numerous restaurants, like two eager and carefree children. Playfulness is a precious quality for sure.

I would have treasured a daughter like Ritzy, someone who is unafraid of being who she is, and who conveys a forthright and genuine expression. Someone who will not give up or forfeit her truth as she dances to the music of life.

How fortunate we are in the course of a lifetime to come across friends that inspire, motivate and elevate our mortal journey.

THE WHITE LOTUS

Raven Zingaro is a Psychic reader in Seattle. Her hair was black like a raven's when I first befriended her. It was blond when I left Seattle.

This transformation reminded me of the Queen of Wands whose dark hair turned golden as she began to know herself on the path of illumination. The fascinating explanation given to me by an East Indian lady many years before was that the Queen of Wands represented a lady of fire who stands strong and steady with a leopard at her side. It is a symbol of great dedication and signifies a gradual understanding of oneself on the journey through life.

Raven seems unafraid of the shadowy darkness or the enmity and greed of human nature. I've seen her stand quiet and strong when hostility is thrown her way. Someone who has the courage to grow and blossom in the most difficult conditions generates a ripple of harmony that affects others in a positive way. Even when thunder and tempestuous winds bluster by this white lotus, she remains unruffled and those fragile petals though bruised, are still intact. Raven is not vociferous, and you may not always see her; if you find her you will be filled with the calm and the deep acceptance that she so generously emanates.

One day when I was concerned about something, Raven said to me: *"Stop worrying, you worry too much!"* Strong yet softly spoken words from a friend, given with the empathetic sword of truth.

Raven is as human as all of us mortals, with emotions and feelings that take us to the depths of despair and the heights of joy. Nevertheless, she's a living example of the commitment and yearning to reach a higher place in our collective human soul journey through this world. Like the white lotus – Raven is quiet and candid.

The lotus grows in pools of water and is mostly hidden below the water level. One has to look into the water to see the strong roots.

I believe that this may be true for all human beings; looking deeper into each person reveals the true strength and courage in all of us. Have we come to expect a mechanically 'fast food' nation where vulnerability is mistaken for weakness? Are humans afraid to look deeper into themselves and each other?

I'm glad to have chanced upon another good friend.

*"The language of friendship
is not words but meanings. "*

~Henry David Thoreau

THE INNOCENCE OF KENNY

Kenny works at Tenzing Momo, an Aladdin's Cave where incense, books, potions and artifacts from India and Tibet are available for purchase. Tenzing Momo is a well-known and established herbal apothecary situated in the historic Pike Place market, in Seattle.

Before working at Tenzing Momo, Kenny used to create floral designs for weddings and events as well as colorful flowering arrangements in prominent hotels all over the Seattle area. He loves flowers.

His childhood years growing up on a farm were filled with incidents and events radiant with the spirit of rural life. I listened eagerly because as he spoke, I felt the veracity of his cheery narrations. Bathed in memories, the warm glow in his face communicated the joys of those years spent on a farm. He befriended farm animals and discovered their unique characteristics. Fascinating stories of animal personalities and their behavior kept us all spellbound and laughing. Kenny spoke with animation and his stories were action-packed. When someone speaks with memories still alive in their heart – it is easy to be immersed in those pictures. It is a living narration.

I was particularly captivated by Kenny's optimistic and affectionate outlook on life as a whole, despite the fact that his partner had died in an accident only two years previously.

Kenny's small back garden in Seattle sounded like Findhorn and after seeing his photos …it looked like Findhorn! His twinkling eyes became alive with delight as he chatted about the healthy red tomatoes growing in his backyard, and flowers emerging into full vivid blooms. He prided himself in taking care of plants as though they were his children.

Big tears welled up in Kenny's eyes when he showed me a photo of Big Polli, the name we fondly used for Erik Pollard, one of our co-workers who had recently died in Prague.

Whenever I chatted with Kenny I was reunited with a breath of innocence. Pure and childlike pleasure is a characteristic not easily found anymore.

*"People from a planet without flowers
would think we must be mad with joy
the whole time
to have such things about us."*

- Iris Murdoch

I'LL SEE YOU AGAIN

I was frequently hired to do handwriting analysis as light entertainment at recreational parties and events in Seattle. One such event was located at an elderly residential home, which was an old and charming building set amongst green trees and colorful gardens. A sense of caring and happiness infused this cheerily flowered place.

Even though I had been hired to give readings to the elderly residents, the smiling and exuberant team of workers came rushing over to my table. Drawn into their enthusiasm and high spirits, I began looking at their writing. They were all friendly and kindhearted people who obviously enjoyed their job in this picturesque setting.

One elderly lady who was an actual resident walked slowly and deliberately over to my table accompanied by her visiting daughter and son-in-law. Her eyes, wide with excitement, maintained a mutually explicit and yet very comfortable visual contact with me. She kept saying: "You're an angel". This naturally made me feel happy and I felt an extraordinary bond with her. After her reading was concluded she went on to say with a knowing smile: *"I'll see you again"*. Without wishing to pore over those words, I replied with profound acknowledgement: *"Yes you will"*.

The feeling persisted that I would see her again. Where, how, why - who knows? I do know that this simple exchange was meaningful to two human beings.

I gave readings to her daughter and son-in-law, both in their seventies and obviously wealthy people; it was undoubtedly the richness of their spirits, all three of them, that captivated my heart in that moment.

I wonder where the spirit of this striking lady resides now, a spirit that shone boldly through clear blue eyes.

I shall always remember that bright face, those lovely sparkling eyes and the words of this ninety eight year old lady:

"I'll see you again"

A MOTHER

Her legs were a little wobbly, her voice eager and questioning as she sat down at the little table and began striking up a conversation.

This eighty-year-old lady made known her state of abject loneliness. A thinly contoured mouth turned downwards as tears welled up in those deep brown eyes. When I asked her to tell me why she felt so abandoned, her answer was short and startling *"My mother just died"* she said.

Stunned at this reply and surely sounding foolish, I tried to find authentic words of comfort. Puzzling over how old her mother must have been, my blank expression and feeble attempts of sympathy seemed to bring on more tears of anguish.

Realizing that she had spent a lifetime – literally with her mother closeby, I knew that her loss was real and poignant.

Numerous people in their twenties, thirties up to their sixties lose their mother; I knew that this lady's sorrow was as justified as everyone else, but I could not imagine how she could have anticipated any other outcome for her mother for at least the last twenty years?

In my perplexed state I forgot to ask her whether she herself had children, grandchildren, or great grandchildren! On the other hand I dared not ask.

The next time I saw her in this café, she told me that she had found solace in the knowledge that her mother was at peace. Watching her hobble away on spindly legs, I was glad to know that her pain was less acute, her grief was easing, and her recognition was taking root in a foundation of acceptance.

THE GARDEN
AND THE CONCRETE

"It's not two, it's One"

These words were one of the diamonds I brought back with me from my visit to Ramesh Balsekar in Bombay, India.

While the intellect may quickly acknowledge wisdom in the form of words, a deep-rooted understanding only occurs through raw experience.

Located in Pike Place Market was one of my favorite coffee shops; it was a place to relax and ponder while gazing out at the mountains over Puget Sound. The cafe was aptly named Sound View. Allowing the warm sun to touch my face through an open window, I noticed some concrete buildings directly facing me – *'They are ugly'* I thought.

On the other hand I was inspired and cheered by the pretty green trees and flowers on somebody's veranda, just a little distance away.

I caught myself judging these two scenes as good or bad, separating the two views by rejecting one picture and praising the other. Ramesh's words came to me very sharply: *"It's not two, it's One" - "It's all God's work."*

Separation creates duality; duality manifests judgments and then we compare. The one we desire while the other we dislike. Ensnared in duality, our human suffering arises as we run from one situation and chase another. As long as humanity denunciates the 'concrete' and glorifies the 'flowers' - the struggle can never end.

Trees, water, mountains in all their natural beauty and color are certainly gifts of life to ease the sometimes-painful journey in this world; I know that I feel soothed by a picturesque landscape and on these afternoons I was reassured and stirred by the flowers.

Humans reach out for the blissful comfort and inspiration of beautiful scenery, but at the same time disliking the 'ugly concrete'. How tempting it is to reject one thing while craving the other in this life; nevertheless, our human condition challenges us to find wholeness in the midst of duality and chaos in the world.

I wish to recognize without disparagement, the concrete and the flowers within the world I live in, within myself and in others. Finding fault in this divine gift of life only fills the heart with discontent.

I wish to find the oneness in all that life offers.

SKIPPING

We go through drama, turmoil and pain.

Why pretend it's not hurting?

It is clearly part of this human incarnation.

OUR human incarnation.

So why not let it be okay?

In true acceptance - there is genuine laughter and joy.

Why not have a 'skipping rope' and have a little 'skip'

when the opportunity is there – no goal in mind…

no formula or technique…

not to rescue or fix or change anything…

not to deny or trivialize the problem

just skipping…

Why not?

SOUL RETRIEVAL

Yet another technique co-opted from the archives of time honored ethnic rituals has burst into the New Age of spirituality. Another buzz word for a new-fangled form of therapy in the arena of modern day society, has been launched.

While living in Seattle I heard numerous enthusiasts claiming how special Soul Retrieval was; as though being told about the latest scintillating restaurant, I remained quietly unconvinced. A designer concept of losing one's soul and then seeking it somewhere, didn't sit well. My trimmed assessment could offend some contemporary soul retrievers as well as a flourishing ensuing market in western society; nonetheless, this is my gutsy opinion. On closer scrutiny, I've personally heard a small number of self-styled therapists positioning themselves as superior seers while using Shamanic techniques. Maybe one of the greatest flaws in this arena is the ability to manipulate those who innocently seek healing and illumination. Has a hopeful and health-seeking sector of the public, handed too much power to quasi 'therapists'? Ultimately, is there ever really a separation? Is who we think we are, only the mind's concept? How do we really lose part of ourselves if there is no separation from Divine Consciousness? What about the wisdom of understanding non-duality and the worthy place it has in healing our human woes?

For the quest of rehabilitation, money is being made from this exploration. It's catching on quickly and schools are popping up where apprentices are being trained in copious rituals from ancient ethnic cultures.

When I aired my views to a friend who had joined one of these institutions of imaginative therapy, she sincerely felt that it had brought about a tremendous amount of clarity and healing in people's lives. She explained that the foundation of Soul Retrieval was rooted in ancient customs derived from the Australian aborigines and Nordic Eskimos. I found myself filled with respect for her sincerity, nonetheless, my personal suspicions were unchanged, especially regarding some entrepreneurial and even idolized 'leaders' of training centers. I once heard a well-respected Indian sage say that it's the honest faith of humble followers of deceptive institutions who emanate that positive transformation, because the purity of their trust creates the alchemy. The charismatic leaders can be the culprits of a misleading idealism, peddled as truth. Have the flourishing founders of modernized and profitable institutions even lived amongst indigenous inhabitants in order to get a glimpse of understanding cultures that have for centuries been steeped in the divine mysteries of their individual faith? By revamping an ancient creed while assimilating it into modern society, a commercial slogan for the latest therapy evolves. Is this not theft of a time honored cultural legacy? It certainly can provide a chaotic, hungry and wealthy society with a 'new toy'.

My academic education in Ethnology was spent amongst fellow students in Zurich, who actually did live amongst indigenous populations in various parts of the world. My Swiss University colleagues felt privileged and humbled by their experience without attempting to exploit the information and knowledge that had been willingly shared. 'New Age' therapists in America and Europe may possibly be lacking in deference; some even misleadingly call themselves 'Cultural Anthropologists'. By using concepts of Australian aborigines as well as Eskimo traditions and translating them into a stylish form of therapy is not a plausible rationale for being a cultural anthropologist. I can't believe that numerous psychic readers and healers have fully understood the nobly, humble and ancient customs that have for centuries, embodied a way of life. Counselors, who demonstrate a lack of humility or an inventive way to assume superiority, will mislead those who sincerely seek healing, knowledge and guidance. Does the general public really fall for restructured buzzwords or a sales pitch that sounds believably elemental?

Are people gullible so as to be falling for chic psychotherapy – and where are the authentic Eskimos and Aborigines? Shouldn't they be consulted before imposters manifestly utilize their time-honored rituals for the purpose of commerce? The original indigenous people may prefer to teach their own rituals – but how can you teach a conscientious and ancient aboriginal custom, which has existed over centuries, to an attention-deficit, modern-day culture? Native cultures have grown up immersed in their way of life from birth – in my opinion they are the only ones who have the authority to teach their own belief system to others. I'm sure that this belief system is not taught in the form of conventional 'lessons' and commercially organized institutions – but is absorbed through daily living and is fundamentally integrated within a natural habitat.

During my scholastic years, I specialized in world religions, Ethno-medicine and Urban Ethnology; writing papers about medicine men and visiting village people in Africa was enlivening and captured my curiosity. While witnessing just a few rituals where the expulsion of bad spirits was explained and demonstrated, I felt humbled and grateful at the kindness of people who unpretentiously opened their hearts and revealed their inherited traditions. I have respected that revelation ever since. As a child growing up in Africa I saw several examples of African rites, which were equally fascinating even then. Sadly, in these current times the voguish grabbing of ethnic rituals in order to commercialize ever more newfangled therapies, is rampant. I would not deem it respectful to ostentatiously invent a mode of therapy based on the remarkable encounters that I was privy to – nor would I presume the right to embody the wisdom of an aboriginal culture. I find this habit of many non-indigenous therapists, to be quite discourteous towards ethnic traditions; this is, of course, my own spirited viewpoint.

To go chasing around after bits of your soul, seems ridiculous to me – if it facilitates people feeling better about life, then it can be viewed as helpful, but why be disingenuous as to assume the knowledge of an ancient race? Admittedly I've had no interest or desire to explore this present-day practice of soul retrieval in depth, because it sounds like another catchword for the latest form of therapy. I'm sure it has its place and value in a transforming society. Thus far however, I'm not convinced.

The soul is eternal - you can't lose it as though it were a pair of gloves! As the Indian Guru Osho was known to say: *'Therapists may often create the need for therapy'*. The concept of a problem can be over-stated, which results in the perceived need to involve an array of therapists. To tell people they have lost bits of their soul and there is a ready-made retriever to help you find it again, is strategic marketing!

This is just one sales pitch by a modern day Shaman: *'Shamanic Healing and Soul Retrieval can assist in attaining life goals, restoring health, releasing old behavioral patterns as well as emotional and psychic pain. It can help relieve symptoms of anxiety, depression, fatigue and stress. Many of my clients find shamanic work immensely helpful in gaining clarity about career, relationship and their soul purpose or life lesson'.*

That sounds very fitting and definitely a good sales pitch for today's ailments. It seems particularly frosty and indifferent to refer to trusting human beings, as 'clients' – I can't imagine that the original shamans saw the people in their tribes as 'clients'. Another quote from a modern day Soul Retriever: *'I help people realize new levels of happiness and fulfillment in a single session'.* The profound search for 'new levels of happiness and fulfillment 'is certainly typical of modern day humanity. A single session – like fast food! Are we as a society ignoring and denying an inherent experience of sorrow and suffering in the world we live in; isn't it part of the world we live in? Surely a loving acceptance of this reality would bring inner peace.

The definition of a Shaman is a practitioner in various small-scale societies, who is believed to be able to diagnose, cure and sometimes cause illness because of a special relationship with, or control over, spirits. Shamanism is based on the belief that invisible forces pervade the visible world. Shamanism requires specialized knowledge or abilities, which are often thought to be obtained through hereditary or supernatural calling.

I'd like to see innovative 'experts' in soul retrieval, being willing to demonstrate a believable authenticity by living with and absorbing the teaching directly from Eskimos and Aborigines, which would embody an unpretentious approach in the healing arena. Or as a friend of mine once said: *"Send them to the Arctic regions – see if these modern money-making soul retrievers can live in an Igloo for a year"*.

One positive result from the embezzlement of a cultural heritage is that it brings some recognition to indigenous societies. Until recently, native philosophies have been derided by a culture that thought of themselves as an elevated species who are superior and even 'civilized'. This recent theft of ethnic rituals, primarily for commercial use, is another assault and oppression. There is a way to make a distinction between those who respectfully attend rituals out of reverence, versus the exploitation for commercial gain.

Without wishing to antagonize the huge fleet of modern day 'soul retrievers' – my intention is to highlight the fact that these traditions do have their rightful place within the wisdom of indigenous cultures!

> *"Once you have heard the meadowlark*
> *and caught the scent of fresh-plowed earth,*
> *peace cannot escape you"*
>
> Sequichie Words of Wisdom by Native Americans

Mailbox in Texas

TEXAS

Bandeira, Texas

MORNING WARMTH

My mother related to me, how her grandfather, Francis Edward Burr (who changed his name to Frank E. Burr once he landed in America), emigrated from England to San Antonio, Texas with his brother William Henry Burr. Their father, Charles Burr, bought his sons a sheep farm in Beeville. Due to a very severe drought, all the animals died. Mum' grandmother used to say: *'The white bones of the Burr sheep were all over Texas'*. The two brothers then made their way to Mexico and worked as civil engineers in the growing oil industry.

Waking up myself in this Texas morning and inhaling the comfortably warm and sultry summer air, there was a sense of being in the tropics. Stepping onto the veranda of our apartment in Indian Hollow, the humid air was a clear indication that I was in San Antonio.

Enjoying the grassy area around the apartment building, the neighborhood dogs were out walking with their humans. Unlike Seattle, humans in this state didn't clean up after their dogs and the ensuing sight and smell of this discourteously 'liberated' approach was off-putting. I saw a strapping young man unleash his dogs for their morning romp in front of our veranda; he proudly spoke about the joys of providing his big dogs with a 'natural environment'. It was a natural environment where flies gathered quickly and greedily in the heat of the day. The majority of dog lovers in Seattle willingly complied with regulations by carrying plastic bags. Even the leash-free parks, of which there were many, were kept hygienic without needing to curtail anyone's freedom. 'Seattle dogs' enjoyed a natural as well as a green and clean environment. It seemed to me that the dog population in San Antonio was rarely treated kindly. There were stray dogs in the city's streets and canine pets were often kept in backyards as an 'alarm system'. During the heat of summer or the freeze of winter, the ones that died were simply replaced with a 'new' one.

While waiting at a bus stop, I came across a young golden Labrador hiding under the seat. When the dog attempted to follow any Latino family he was consistently kicked and sent away – people were more concerned about chatting on their cell phones. On seeing a parked police car nearby, I went over to let the officer know this dog was a stray and was in danger of being killed on the busy road – or even causing an accident. Sadly the burly Latino officer would not speak to me or bother with the time involved in this issue. He turned his face away and boorishly ignored my effort to catch his attention or appeal for his help. The cop stealthily watched me walk over to Burger King to purchase food for the dog. The young Hispanic servers at Burger King were also indifferent to the predicament of a stray dog and unflinchingly charged me the full price for all three burgers for this skeletal and very hungry dog. My husband came to pick me up in the car and we drove the dog to a nearby animal shelter only to find they wouldn't take the good-natured animal. With a feeble explanation that the dog was flea infested and too big – and that they were: 'full and could only take small dogs who were not flea infested'. After being told to take him to a different animal shelter, we drove for another forty-five minutes across this city. The other alternative offered to us was to drop him off on the street where we found him! I began to wonder what kind of city this was where litter was being thrown around on streets and roadsides – was I in a 'backward' country where animals were often treated with disdain and cruelty and debris was being thrust around without respect or pride for the upkeep of this city.

I liked the noisy wildlife in Texas, where birds sang loudly and raucously amongst the trees as the cool respite of evening approached; bird songs mingled with the sound of invisible crickets and it was always a busy night for them. Even the natural world was brazen here in cowboy land. Perhaps they were competing with human noises.

During the month of June, days are hot, becoming even hotter as August approaches. There's no ocean within two hours, yet initially I found myself enjoying the change from Seattle. After a couple of years, the scorching heat of summer and the dusty roadside bus stops, where huge motor vehicles appropriately named SUV's roared by me while audaciously flouting any speed limits - began to drain my energy greatly. I felt a deep understanding for my mother who was so exhausted by the heat on the East African continent, as we were growing up in close proximity to the Equator.

As the cars sped around like bullies in San Antonio, they effectively ignored speed limits or even traffic lights. I saw a dead armadillo on the road after being hit by a car and left to rot - it was covered in flies. Road rules were blatantly disregarded as lively faces racing around with abandon in bulky macho four-wheel drive vehicles could be seen chatting and laughing on cell phones. We avoided accidents on numerous occasions when someone in another vehicle continued their phone chat.

This must be Texas!

A prominent politician said: *'Don't mess with Texas!'* Okay……. *I won't mess with Texas.* I also heard a lot of Texans proudly stating: *'I want my freedom'*. I silently questioned their dependence on cars – while clearly recognizing that public transport was not easy in San Antonio and teenagers seemed to procure a car as soon as they could drive. Is that really freedom? Is it freedom to throw trash out of car windows - is that the freedom they speak about?

CRASH

"If there are no expectations,
then you are free.
If you expect, then you are in bondage.
Choose whatever you want.
Expectations are rarely fulfilled."

Poonjaji

I recently saw a movie called 'Crash'. The film was about racial and social tensions in Los Angeles, California. Several characters' stories interweave during two days in Los Angeles. Rather than separating the characters into victims and offenders, victims of racism are often shown to be racist themselves in different contexts and situations. Also, racist remarks and actions are often shown to stem from ignorance and misconception rather than a malicious personality.

Intensely filled with the disturbing kaleidoscope of human emotions, anyone watching the movie must be powerfully stirred by the implications.

Habitually ingrained into a reactive impulse, the human mind is filled with assumptions and attitudes based upon past encounters. Fear, pain and anger accumulate into a knee jerk reaction. A need and capacity to fully understand these instinctive emotions, can ease our tenuous and human state.

Judgments made about skin color, race, age, attire, speech, caste and class are responses based on a 'conditioned past' where the mind is programmed into a specific belief pattern. Is this the state of humanity now? Suspicious, angry and fearful? No I think not, because, as the movie illustrated so brilliantly – the qualities of love, forgiveness and humor were also incorporated into the profound network of human interaction. A response based on a fresh look at the present situation is the key and the way to clean the slate of a distressing past.

This movie directly incorporated the depth and intensity of an individual's behavior and awareness – can we really be principled in judging the whole world of another person – is self-righteousness the consequence of a shallow evaluation of our fellow human beings? Neatly labeled suppositions can be made about a person, based on small-minded and uncalled-for reasons.

I believe that each and every one of us has suffered the hurt of being mis-understood; it creates a desire in the injured party to be guarded and only say what may please others – for fear of being misinterpreted.

I would love to glimpse a world where humanity can acknowledge and see beyond the words and actions of other people; to even feel the pain and hurt that causes another person to react and take certain measures. I am asking a lot of humanity, and yet I believe it is possible.

Rising into a higher place where compassion, love and forgiveness are given to oneself and to others, is the place I speak of.

"Be kind
For everyone you meet
is fighting a hard battle"

When life seems utterly overwhelming –

"KEEP BREATHING

AND SEE WHAT THE TIDE BRINGS IN"

(From the movie 'Castaway')

DISAPPOINTMENT

"Hope is a waking dream"
Aristotle

Filled with unconquerable plans that point to apparent success, we mortals surf on a wave of optimism. Flying high with hope and determination and energized by the vision of achievement – life is sparkling with future endeavors!

That crash of disillusionment is devastating when dreams smash to the ground in an explosion of presumed failure. It is confidence busting to say the least. What if……… why……….I should have……….I could have…………the pain of self-torment commences with a desire to place blame on oneself or some other person. It's not effortless to simply accept the ache of loss and to walk on with self-respect and composure.

How many times have you felt disappointed? Reflecting back on that or any other painful episode – were they really disappointments?

Someone once said that our individual existence is not separate to the lives of all living things. Each and every fiber of life blends together to create a painting or an embroidered work of art, each individual thread of color merges in accordance with a divine arrangement. How then, can we assume to be in rigid control of our own separate path? A single thread has no choice but to surrender in dignity and awe at the greater picture while sacrificing an insistently indomitable drive towards self-satisfaction and even personal gain. Firmly attached to our individual agenda while ignoring Life's more expanded vision, is a recipe for personal disaster. Nevertheless, the snare of wielding our own willpower, thinking it will bring fulfillment is enticing.

When filled with the purity of unpretentious wisdom, a sincerely joyful urge to manifest dreams and aspirations is heartwarming. The vision itself is not the burden; it is a clutching attachment filled with need and fear, that usually creates the uptight and brittle sense of power.

As the rough cut diamond is polished and smoothed through painful and abrasive buffing, so the layers of our headstrong ego drop away to reveal the pure shining diamond of awareness.

My friend Diana S. sent me this quote:

"I listen to the wind rustle the leaves, it calms me, but calm is not the only song the wind sings. Tornado, hurricane, cyclone wind bringing blizzard roaring over earth, ripping vines, flattening fields of green; wind fanning the flames of forest fires; wind lifting the ocean's waves, twisting trees – these winds also sing.

It is said that God speaks only in the gentle breeze, that is untrue, spirita sancta is the wind of God, she blows as hard as need be, she sweeps through, uprooting dead thoughts, she blows new life like a whirlwind, she whirls into my heart, she clears a space in my mind.

There are times I gritted my teeth, determined to get through whatever life has dealt.

Endurance is not like that, people break when they are too hard. Endurance is like a river – it is liquid, it surrounds obstacles, washes them away or it dissolves them. Endurance is the deep flow under the ice of winter; it is the shallow flow continuing through the years of drought carving rivulets through clay. Endurance sculpts the canyon and the gorge; it uncovers lost and buried beauty"

We mortals have the choice to give our hearts totally to whatever we do in our life, though the outcome may not be in our hands - the journey is! Surely it is the way we walk our path in life that fulfills our human soul? The actual goals, whether one reaches them or not, may not be as fulfilling as anticipated.

"He who embraces the dawn of truth with his inner eyes, will ever be ecstatic, like the murmuring brook".

KAHLIL GIBRAN 'Secrets of the Heart'

YOLANDA'S NEW SHOES

There was a friendly welcome on that first day I arrived as a front desk agent at this picturesque luxury hotel. With smiling brown eyes and an even-tempered nature, Yolanda's innate ability to include each person in a friendly rapport was inspiring to anyone who began training under her patient and caring guidance. Having attained a Master's degree in hotel management, her qualified credentials exceeded most of her peers at the front office and yet her approach was egalitarian and fair, never once espousing her managerial position as a way to demonstrate power. Yolanda truly loved her job and this was obvious in the meticulous and thorough way she went about her work as well as genuine warmth she extended to guests and fellow associates. The practical and human aspect of this twenty six year old young woman was immediately impressive. Where others in their youthful twenties may attempt to emphasize 'cool' behavior or engage in self-important and deriding gossip as a way to boost their own status, Yolanda maintained a true graciousness towards all who came her way. She had the strength of character to make her own estimations of each situation and a professional adeptness at problem solving. She gained the respect and affection of those who worked with her, except for a very few who seemed spitefully envious of her skills and friendly personality.

I will always remember that first day when her animated face was alive with excitement at the prospect of an upcoming trip to Las Vegas: *"I'm so excited about going to Las Vegas,"* she said.

Drawn into the warmth of her openhanded stance, I felt thrilled about her trip and shared my own prior experiences of that colorful desert city. I told her about the tea at Bellagio where shiny silver teapots contained the most wonderful tea. Colored fountains of water that dance to music held me spellbound! I had been enthralled by the make-believe cities of Paris and Venice in Las Vegas.

Even in those early days, Yolanda's inherent ability to actually hear what another person is saying was obvious – not just the words but the whole perspective in which words are expressed. For someone so young, she exhibited rare qualities of wisdom and an instantly recognizable credibility.

Yolanda was looking at a mail order catalogue one evening while the front desk was quiet, our work was up to date and we were relaxed. I was drawn into the cheerful venture of looking at adorable and practical shoes; moreover, I felt touched at being included in this friendly browsing. It was like going on a shopping trip with a friend. Yolanda didn't shut people out.

She took time to choose her shoes; it was not a greedy grabbing approach but a process that evolved with thoughtfulness. Her enjoyment and the attention to detail surrounding this 'shopping trip' was inspiring to me.

When she came to work wearing the new black shoes, her bright face was alight. Having also participated in this venture, I felt elated to see the shiny footwear.

Yolanda's parents, who came to Texas from Mexico many years before, were not only hard working but were devoted to their children. I felt a profound admiration for two people who had made sure their four children had a principled and confident start in life where self-worth and respect are considered to be far-reaching values. Without having even met them, I respected their courage. I have always had a high regard for anyone who lives life in the face of harsh challenges. It heartens and motivates me in my own struggles when I hear about those who have overcome difficulties in their life.

Yolanda's parents were in my age group, which gave me a further understanding - they had lived the same amount of years that I had. It gave me a profound insight into someone else's life journey.

I enjoyed those quiet evenings when Yolanda would talk about her parents and the remarkable life journey they had experienced. Yolanda was also a skilled and creative jewelry maker. When she brought her hand crafted earrings for me to see, I was astounded at the workmanship and colors that had gone into elaborate and imaginative designs. I learnt so much about this city and the hotel environment during our chats, which added to the contentment of the work.

Yolanda didn't single out or ostracize anyone; in her eyes, age, race or gender were not valid reasons to snub anybody. I was older than my fellow workers at the front desk, and my sensitive nature caused me to take some conjectures a little too personally, when in reality I could have been less thin-skinned! I learnt from that experience.

Yolanda actually listened to people – her open mind and receptive heart certainly had a healing effect on me in a time of vulnerability. I had made a good friend.

Living in San Antonio, memories of my mother reminiscing about Mexico City where she was born, came flooding back. Having lived there as a child amongst other European settlers, my mother was very drawn to the Latino character traits herself. I felt connected to my mother in this lively Hispanic society. I enjoyed bus rides to the city where mature and friendly faces met me and offers of help were abundant when I needed directions. In the heat of those first summer months, while chatting with a dark haired cheerful lady on the bus, I was advised to use an umbrella to protect from the scorching sun; I felt heartened by her kindness. I saw young women on the bus, on their way to work with small children. Their faces were filled with the strength of endurance. I initially felt welcomed by a Hispanic society who worked hard, had a smile on their face and expressed a likable spirit of kinship.

On occasions I was puzzled by a portion of the younger generation of 'San Antonions' who seemed to scowl and had little interest or pride in their work. A young generation who felt that society owed them something. Like any country and any city, there is a mixture of personalities – in this city there seemed to be a small and emerging stratum of contemptuous youth who didn't seem to like Caucasians very much. Was this a reaction? Did they feel that their parents had been treated disdainfully by a previous generation of Americans? The Hispanic culture has a proud and great ethnic history and being a keen student of sociology, this apparent growing sullenness displayed by Latino youth towards Caucasians in the area, puzzled me. I was also uneasy by this choice of unconcealed division.

MARSHMALLOWS

I love marshmallows!

That melting sensation of gentle euphoria glows warmly through my senses as I munch on a soft cloud of sugary fluff. Endomorphins activate brain activity, creating sensations of happiness as marshmallow meets taste buds in a dulcet synthesis of pleasure. Disappointingly, this sensation comes to an abrupt end once the last sweet remnant has gone, moving on its fated journey where it gleefully adds calories and adipose tissue to the body.

When the last morsel of marshmallow is consumed, an empty sense of yearning strives for attention - is that 'cold-turkey'?

Even though I might enjoy the prospect of a never-ending 'marshmallow sensation', I'm nevertheless very appreciative of this fleeting moment of delight.

Allegorically speaking, once the marshmallow has been savored one could spend a lifetime longing for or indulging in the enticing world of euphoric bonbons, perhaps even imagining this to be the remedy and the solution to those bleak sensations of emptiness. Indeed after a perceived glimpse of spiritual enlightenment, I've seen human beings ensnared in an unrelenting and even agitated longing for Nirvana – which is certainly not a bad craving except when the seeking also becomes an addiction. Or on the more earthly level - the addiction to material possessions and wealth can be a pitiful form of incarceration. I chuckled when I heard a renowned movie star say that the sumptuous land of Monaco could be compared to an 'Alcatraz for the rich'.

A wise sage once said that mankind has a tendency to want to keep repeating happy sensations by re-visiting that moment in the past, without fully accepting that the past is finished and each new moment offers the spontaneous regenerative mystery of a fresh dawn. The desire for human nature to duplicate past idyllic events and get stuck in a desire to re-live that happy sensation eliminates the realistic discernment that it was originally born of the unfathomable and present moment. One could also become trapped in the frozen memory of a past event whether it was pleasant or not.

By excessively indulging in a consoling assortment of miscellany, an unrestrained desire to be numbed into comatose passivity can be an enticing escape from reality – especially when life becomes painfully challenging.

Certainly as children, the sweet comfort of candy can fill a lonely void where love and joy may be missing at this vulnerable time in life. That edibly addictive solace and the need for affection in childhood may evolve into adulthood as a craving for 'comfort foods', in the hope of bringing ultimate contentment. Alas, this short-lived simulated cure can only fuel and not satisfy the hunger for true comfort. On the other hand – the innocently unfettered enjoyment of candy by children and adults alike is genuinely rewarding without the ensnarement by an uncontrollable allure.

The attempt to fill an empty and perhaps lonely place in one's individual world with a gratifying sweetie is not without consequences. Wisdom, strength, hope and emotional maturity are the trusty tools in this precarious dilemma. The nurturing revival of self-esteem, self-awareness and quiet acceptance are qualities born of courage, at which time the marshmallow becomes a pleasantly relaxed delicacy instead of an unrestrained, irresistible and compulsive craving. Surely the measured choice to take pleasure in a marshmallow is better than submitting to an overpowering and wild craving? It's the difference between emancipation and bondage.

I love marshmallows!

NOAH'S ARK

In 2005, it occurred to me that the story of Noah's ark is not history being retold but the future being prophesized. All the animals loaded into the ark 'two by two' are really DNA samples being collected by worried scientists and politicians, who may be busy doing this right now? Indeed I now hear in 2014, that scientists have recently been speaking about this very issue

In symbolic language understandable to humans, well over two thousand years ago, the concept of Noah's Ark, the flood and the animals being chosen in pairs may have been drawn on to demonstrate that the planet Gaia, as a living healthy organism needs to cleanse itself. The planet characteristically needs to maintain its continued existence.

When humans choose to live in unison with the earth, an ensuing and mutual nurturing takes place.

I am not sure that the humans in authority have ever chosen to respect this planet or even whether past lessons have been learnt through dreadful blunders – even though ancient literature reveals numerous incidents where humans have brutally and continually abused each other and the earth we live in.

I wonder why the human brain may have not figured out the consequence of certain actions. Perhaps greed and the lure of instant pleasure is a stronger instinct than a slower path towards harmony and unity.

"There are those that look at things the way they are, and ask why.
I dream of things that never were, and ask, why not?"

Robert Kennedy

EPILOGUE

My narratives continue to be written, but for now I'm closing with the most recent story 'Noah's Ark'.

Putting thoughts in writing and escaping into this creative world is a labor of love and I am hugely appreciative of the lap top computer, which has become a friend. Whether or not my writing venture becomes a means of financial support, it has certainly given me many hours of fulfilling solace and companionship.

I feel soothed and grateful for the opportunity, not only as a means of expression but also to share heartfelt observations. By losing myself in writing - I find myself.

I write in the hope of reaching others who share the spirit of community that I so value. A wise spiritual teacher who was dying, said these words: *"I leave you my dream..."*

This is what we all do in this life; we leave behind us an imprint of the very core of our existence – our dream. Writing can be a witness to our life. A family is a witness to our life.

I've given up the idea of trying to understand or find logic in the hand of fate, though I have often felt upset with 'it'. How true those words that I heard many years ago: *"If you don't willingly walk the path predestined for you, you will be pushed along it!"*

Though we are unique individuals, there are shared feelings and thoughts as a universal human legacy – when someone reveals their individual reflections in the form of writing, an affinity that strikes a chord of understanding can lighten a world that is sprinkled with misunderstanding and aloneness. Perhaps reading and writing is the hope of alliance with other human beings.

"As the Lotus does not touch the water,
           So do not let the world
           Disturb your heart.
      Being busy in the world is no trouble
     Unless you are troubled by being busy.
      Then the only trouble is the trouble."

*"Legends say that hummingbirds float free of time,
carrying our hopes for love, joy and celebration.
The hummingbird's delicate grace reminds us
that life is rich, beauty is everywhere.
Every personal connection has meaning
and laughter is life's sweetest creation"*

Scott Leland (Atmo Ram) named me 'Hummingbird flower'

Photo by Ritzy Ryciak

Charmiene Maxwell-Batten was born in Devon, England in the small town of Axminster. At six weeks old she left for Uganda, with her parents and brother Jonathan. Charmiene's father was embarking on a career as a government inspector and consultant in the coffee industry on the East African continent.

Charmiene and her brother lived in Kampala for almost ten years as the family grew; those were joyful events when our brother Justin and sister Margherita were born at Entebbe hospital in Kampala. Later when the family returned to England, Dominic our youngest sibling was born in Dorset.

Charmiene has a profound interest in Natural health, alternative medicine, herbal remedies as well as an early and creative passion for ballet and writing, which has continued throughout her life. Her entrance into Zurich University to study for a degree in Ethnology was both rewarding and enriching.

Her many years in Switzerland, India, Thailand and USA have provided a deep appreciation for cultural diversity; visiting three spiritual teachers in India have enhanced an understanding of our inner as well as a mortal human journey in this world. In 1992 she was inspired to write and share her experiences.

Charmiene's paternal great grandfather, Reverend Sabine Baring-Gould, the author of the well-known hymns 'Onward Christian Soldiers' and 'Now the Day is Over', was also an avid traveler and major literary figure, who was an authority on myths, legends and folklore. Baring-Gould was a friend and literary peer of George Bernard Shaw and Arthur Conan Doyle. His marriage to Grace Taylor was the basis of the character Eliza Doolittle in Pygmalion. Rumor has it that that his estate Lew Trenchard Manor in Dartmoor, provided the atmosphere and setting for Conan Doyle's 'Hound of the Baskervilles'. Baring Gould also appears as a character in Laurie King's Sherlock Holmes novel – 'The Moor'.

Sabine Baring-Gould

Charmiene at Lew Trenchard Manor 1993

Beautiful Dartmoor

"Do you see how every little breath of wind that sighed against the shore, was written down? The record of the weeping skies is brought to light; and now that which was hidden is revealed. He who has written these down on tables of stone, must have recorded the tears which fall on the earth and which to many, are unknown"

Sabine Baring-Gould
From his book 'The Mystery of Suffering'

I wonder whether my great grandfather felt lonely and often misunderstood – as I read his books written over a century ago, I'm profoundly touched by the insight and awareness. I even wonder if today he is fully appreciated for all his written work. Besides the acclaim for having written the hymn 'Onward Christian Soldiers' – his capacity for depth and understanding should stir the consciousness and soul of any spiritual seeker today.

Charmiene Maxwell-Batten